MW00654036

TRAILER
TRASH
COOKIN'

by Rick Black

About The Author

Rick Black is a veteran hunter, fisherman, and outdoor cook. He has written several wild game cookbooks and how-to books on hunting.

Rick's books seem to attract hunters like doe urine on a fresh scrape. His books are entertaining, with great recipes and humorous short stories.

Rick is very active in many state and regional outdoor associations and has served as President/Sergeant of a local police department reserve unit, and is a proud longtime N.R.A. member.

Although the fall and winter months are a busy time for Rick, he still makes several radio appearances and book signings. Rick loves talking and swapping hunting stories and recipes with his readers.

He and his wife, Becky, are longtime residents of southeast Iowa.

For information on scheduling Rick for your outdoor organization and fund raisings, call the publisher's 800 number on the back of this book.

Dedication

This book is dedicated to my late friend Larry "Chopper" Krueger.
Chopper took a chance 25 years ago, on a wild 18-year-old red neck country boy and co-signed for his first real loan when everyone else thought that kid would never stop his hunting and fishing to buckle down and get a real job.

Well, I proved all those people wrong; I paid Chopper back in full! Chopper had a double wide in the middle of nowhere Iowa, and although it was small, Chopper always had room at his table for a friend.

Chopper was one of the funniest men I ever met. He was a true friend to all!

Rest In Peace Cousin Larry
Rick

Foreword

"I want to go on record that I think this book is tasteless and despicable. I absolutely love it!"

- Kent Ball
Fishing buddy, Buford S.C.

"I have no idea why my daughter puts up with this man!

- My Mother-In-Law

Introduction

If I only had a dollar for every time I heard the sound of my wife's voice screaming " *Why must you drag all them trailer trash buddies of yours to our house and drink beer!"* Yep it is the same thing every weekend when we are not out huntin' or fishin'.

So how did I get my lovely bride of over 19 years to put up with this?
Well, ...I didn't. You see Becky just can't understand the views and philosophies of my trailer court comrades.

I think this could be solved if she only understood the meaning of duct tape, cars in the driveways with the hood up, on blocks holding the front axle because of missing tires.

I think it all started when she found a love letter Bubba wrote five years ago to the lady in the trailer next to his. We call her the cat lady because she always wants us to go over and pet her kitty, but she don't have no cat? Anyways it went like this:

Kudzu is green, my dog's name is Blue,
And I'm so lucky to have a sweet thang like you.
Yore hair is like cornsilk, a-flappin' in the breeze.
Softer than Blue's, and without all them fleas.
You move like the bass, which excites me in May.
You ain't got no scales, but I luv you anyway.

You're as graceful as okry, jist a-dancin' in the pan.
Yore as fragrant as SunDrop, right out of the can.

You have all yore teeth, for which I am proud;
I hold my head high when we're in a crowd.

On special occasions when you shave yore armpits,
Well, I'm in hawg heaven! Plumb outta my wits!
And speakin' of wits, you're got plenty fer shore.
'Cuz you keep the same hairstyle from '74.

Still them fellers at work, they all want to know,
What I did to snag me such a purty young doe.
Like a good roll of duct tape, yore there fer yore man,
To patch up life's troubles, and stick 'em in the can.

Yore as strong as a four-wheeler racin' through the mud,
Yet fragile as that sanger, named Naomi Judd.
Yore as cute as a junebug, a-buzzin' overhead.
You ain't mean like no far ant, upon which I oft' tread.

Cut from the best pattern like a flannel shirt of plaid,
You sparked up my life, like a Rattletrap shad.

When you hold me real tight, like a padded gunrack,
My life is complete; ain't nuttin' I lack.
Yore complexion, it's perfection, like the best vinyl sidin'.
Despite all the years, yore age it keeps hidin'.

And when you get old like a '57 Chevy,
Won't put you on blocks, and let grass grow up heavy.
Me 'n' you's like a Moon Pie, with a RC cold drank;
We go together, like a skunk goes with stank.

Some men, they buy chocolate, for Valentine's Day;
They git it at Wal-Mart; it's romantic that way.
Some men git roses on that special day, from the cooler at Kroger; "That's impressive," I say.

Some men buy fine diamonds, from a flea market booth.
"Diamonds are forever," they explain, suave and couth.

But for this man, honey, these will not do.

For you are too special, you sweet thang you.
I got you a gift, without taste nor odor,
Better than diamonds—it's a new trollin' motor!

Luv your step-brother,
BUBBA

Well that's it folks, now you know what has inspired me to write this cookbook. Not just for Becky, but also for the whole world to better understand Traylor Trash Cookin'!

Enjoy!
Cousin Rick

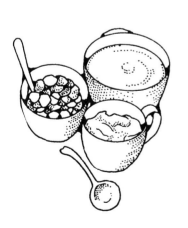

Recipes With Government Issued Pork With Natural Juices.
(SPAM Or TREET)

Hum, hum, when it comes to the government issued Pork With Natural Juices (Known as monkey meat or SPAM Meat) ain't nothin' better fer the youngons' and you!

So kick back and down a cold one, this chapter is fer' the little heifer, the rug rats, and you!

The First Of The Month Party
Sandwiches -

- 2 (1-pound) un-sliced loaves Italian bread
- 1 (8-ounce) package cream cheese, softened
- 1 cup shredded (Government Issued) cheese
- $\frac{3}{4}$ cup sliced green onions
- $\frac{1}{4}$ cup mayonnaise
- 1 tablespoon Worcestershire sauce
- 1 pound thinly, sliced SPAM
- 1 pound thinly sliced (Government Canned) beef
- 12 thin slices dill pickle

Cut the bread in half lengthwise. Hollow out top and bottom of loaves, leaving a $\frac{1}{2}$ inch shell.

Combine the cheese, onions, mayonnaise, and Worcestershire sauce; spread over cut slices of bread.

Layer Spam and beef on bottom and top halves; place the pickles on the bottom halves.
Gently press the halves together. Wrap in plastic wrap and refrigerate for at least two hours.

Thank God Fer' Democrats Government Pork & Onion Casserole –

- 3 large thinly sliced onions
- 1 can cream of celery soup
- $\frac{1}{2}$ pound Government pork

Preheat oven to 350 degrees. Place the onions in casserole dish. Lay pork over onions and pour soup over all.

Bake fer' about an hour and serve vittles when hot.

Free Cheese Delight -

- 2 cups warm milk
- 2 cans Spam, diced
- 1 cup breadcrumbs
- 1 teaspoon Worcestershire sauce
- 1 tablespoon paprika
- 1 cup grated cheese
- ½ teaspoon mustard
- 1 egg, beaten
- 1 teaspoon salt

Combine all ingredients and bake at 350 degrees fer' about an hour.

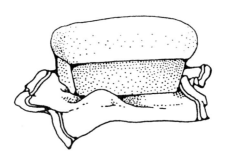

Pull My Finger Broccoli Chowder –

- 1 pounds fresh broccoli
- 1 ½ cups chicken broth
- 1 ½ cups grated cheese
- ½ cup chopped Spam
- ½ teaspoon salt
- ½ teaspoon pepper
- 1 ½ cups milk
- 2 tablespoons butter (government issued)

Wash broccoli; remove leaves and stem ends.
Pour broth in a large pot.
Bring to boil, add the broccoli and reduce heat.
Simmer fer' about 5 minutes, uncovered, then
cover and cook fer' about 10 more minutes, until
the broccoli is tender.

Remove broccoli with a slotted spoon; chop into
bite-size pieces, add milk, Spam, salt, and pepper
to stock.
Bring to boil, stirring often. Stir in cheese,
butter and broccoli and heat until the cheese is
melted.

Who Cut The Cheese? Sandwiches -

- 1 can sliced pork (government issued)
- 2 tablespoons butter (government issued)
- $\frac{1}{2}$ pound sliced cheese (government issued)
- Salt, pepper, and bread

Melt butter in a large frying pan and fry up the pork until brown.

Slap on the cheese and let it melt. Salt and pepper to your licking, and serve on bread.

Trailer Trash Tips

Personal Hygiene:

- ➤ Unlike clothes and shoes, a toothbrush should never be a hand-me-down item.

- ➤ If you have to vacuum the bed, it's time to change the sheets.

- ➤ While ears need to be cleaned regularly, this is a job that should be done in private using one's OWN truck keys.

- ➤ Plucking unwanted nose hair is time-consuming work. A cigarette lighter and a small tolerance for pain can accomplish the same goal and save hours. NOTE: It's a good idea to keep a bucket of water handy when using this method.

Dining Out:

➤ Remember to leave a generous tip fer' good service. After all, their trailer costs just as much as yours.

➤ Keep in mind most truck stops don't take food stamps fer' a meal...the key word here is MOST.

➤ Swapin' spit with your date while waitin' fer' your meal to come is sometimes frond upon. So tell your stepsister to settle down!

➤ Do not buy your vittles with food stamps and ask the cook at the truck stop to "Fix us up a mean mess of hash".

➤ Do not squeeze the zit on your dates back, even if the "over-the-shoulder-boobie-holder" doesn't cover it!

Tips Fer' all occasions:

- Never take a beer to a job interview or ask if they press charges.

- Always say, "Excuse me" after getting sick in someone else's car.

- The socially refined never fish coins out of public toilets, especially if other people are around.

- Always provide an alibi to the police for family members.

- When dancing, never remove undergarments, no matter how hot it is.

- Crying babies should be taken to the lobby and picked up immediately after the movie has ended.

➤ Refrain from talking to your T.V. screen. Tests have proven the characters can't hear you.

➤ Never "lite up a fart" in public. This should be done at home or in your car.

➤ If your dog falls in love with a guest's leg, have the decency to leave them alone for a few minutes.

➤ If you are using the broken down Chevy in your yard as an office to sell night crawlers, always put the worms on ice. Ice can be bought with food stamps. Note: If it is during the middle of the month and you don't have any food stamps left because you traded them fer' beer and smokes, you can always steal the ice from the local motel ice machine.

We Livin' Large Casserole –

- 12 eggs
- 2 pounds diced Spam
- 10 ounces sliced mushrooms
- 1 can cream of mushroom soup
- $\frac{1}{2}$ cup milk
- 10 ounces shredded cheese
- 12-pack beer (For you to drink while cookin')

Mix the eggs with milk and mushrooms, scramble and put in a large casserole dish.

Layer diced Spam on eggs. Warm soup in a pan and pour over meat and top with cheese.

Bake at 250 degrees fer' about 35 minutes covered, then 30 more minutes uncovered.

NOTE: You can't buy beer with food stamps. You will have to trade for it!

Crock-Pot Crap –

- 1 cup diced Spam
- 1 cup butter
- 1 cup chopped onion
- 2 cups chopped celery
- 12 cups breadcrumbs
- 1 teaspoon seasoning salt
- 1 teaspoon pepper
- 1 teaspoon sage
- 5 cups chicken stock
- 3 beaten eggs
- 1 large can mushrooms

Cook the celery and onions in butter until tender. Add the celery and onions with all the remaining ingredients and place in the crock-pot.

Cook in crock-pot on low fer' about 8 hours.

Boogie Bake -

- 14 ounce box Minute Rice
- 1 can cream of cheddar soup
- 1 can cream of mushroom soup
- 2 cans cream of chicken soup
- 16 ounce package frozen chopped broccoli
- 1 quart milk
- 8 cans Spam, sliced

Grease a large casserole dish. Combine the first six ingredients and pour into dish.

Top with Spam and press meat into the mixture. Cover and bake at 350 degrees for about 90 minutes.

Sauerkraut

- 6 cans chopped Spam
- 1 small head of cabbage, thinly sliced
- 1 onion, thinly sliced
- 1 teaspoon dill weed
- 1 cup water
- 3 cans sauerkraut
- 1 teaspoon caraway seed
- 1 teaspoon salt
- 1 teaspoon garlic powder

Brown the meat in a skillet. In a large crock-pot layer meat, sauerkraut, cabbage, and onion.

Add the caraway seed, garlic powder, salt, pepper, dill weed, and water.

Cover and cook on low heat fer' about 8 hours. Stir several times while cooking.

Gimmie' Some Of That Good Lovin' Skillet Dinner –

- 3 cans sliced Spam
- 2 cans cream of mushroom soup
- 4 potatoes, thick sliced
- 1 can drained green beans
- 1 can drained mushrooms
- $\frac{1}{2}$ cup milk
- 2 cups chopped carrots
- 1 teaspoon salt
- 1 teaspoon pepper
- 1 teaspoon garlic powder

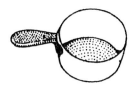

In a large skillet, brown Spam in butter. Remove meat, drain fat, and return meat back to skillet.

Mix the remaining ingredients together and pour over meat.

Simmer until the taters' are done.

Talkin' Trailer Trash

➤ Two trailer park dudes are walking toward each other, and one is carrying a sack. When they meet, one says, "Hey Tommy Ray, whatcha got in th' bag?" "Jes' some chickens." "If I guesses how many they is, kin I have one?" "Shoot, if ya guesses right, I'll give you both of 'em!" "OK. Ummmmm...five?"

➤ Ida Mae passed away and Bubba called 911. The 911-operator told Bubba that she would send someone out right away. "Where do you live?" asked the operator. Bubba replied, "Number 7 at Eucalyptus Traylor Court." The operator asked, "Can you spell that for me?" After a long pause, Bubba said, "How 'bout I drag her over to Oak Street and you pick her up there?"

TRAILER TRASH MEDICAL TERMS:

Benign - *What you be after you be eight.*

Bacteria - *Back door to cafeteria.*

Barium - *What doctors do when patients die.*

Cesarean Section - *A neighborhood in Rome.*

Cat scan – *Searching for kitty.*

Cauterize – *Made eye contact with her.*

Colic – *A sheep dog.*

Coma – *A punctuation mark.*

D&C – *Where Washington is.*

Dilate – *To live long.*

Enema – *Not a friend.*

Fester – *Quicker than someone else.*

Fibula – *A small lie.*

G.I. Series – *World Series of military baseball.*

Hangnail – *What you hang your coat on.*

Impotent – *Distinguished, well known.*

Labor Pain – *Getting hurt at work.*

Medical Staff – *A doctor's cane.*

Morbid – *A higher offer than I bid.*

Nitrates – *Cheaper than day rates.*

Node – *I knew it.*

Pelvis – *Second cousin to Elvis.*

Pap Smear – *A fatherhood test.*

Post Operative – *The man that bring us the welfare checks.*

Recovery Room – *Place to do upholstery.*

Rectum – *Damn near killed him.*

Secretion – *Hiding something.*

Seizure – *Roman emperor.*

Tablet – *A small table.*

Terminal Illness – *Getting sick at the airport.*

You're Trailer Trash If:

➢ You belch after a good meal rather than say your compliments to the chef.

➢ You have more than three broken down Chevys in your yard.

➢ You let your 13 year old daughter smoke at the table in front of HER kids.

➢ You take your dog for a walk and you both use the same tree.

➢ Your property has been mistaken for a recycling center.

- You burn your yard rather than mow it.

- The Salvation Army declines your mattress.

- You come back from the dump with more than you took.

- You keep a can of RAID on the kitchen table.

- You find your dates at the V.D. clinic.

- Your trailer doesn't have curtains but your truck does.

- Your father executes the "Pull my finger" trick during Christmas dinner.

- You wonder how service stations keep their restrooms so clean.

➤ You can spit without opening your mouth.

➤ You consider your license plate personalized because your father made it.

➤ Your lifetime goal is to own a night crawler stand.

➤ You have a complete set of salad bowls and they all say COOL WHIP on the side.

➤ Your working TV sits on top of your non-working TV.

➤ A tornado hits your trailer park and does $100,000 worth of improvement.

Casserole –

- 1 can undrained kernel corn
- 1 can cream style corn
- $\frac{1}{2}$ stick butter
- $\frac{1}{2}$ cup chopped green onions
- $\frac{1}{2}$ cup chopped green peppers
- 1 box cornbread mix
- 1 cup shredded cheese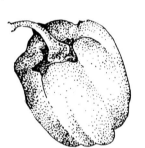
- 1 cup chopped Spam
- 2 eggs
- 1 cup sour cream
- 1 teaspoon garlic salt
- 1 teaspoon black pepper

Melt the butter; beat in the eggs and sour cream.

Mix in the remaining ingredients into a large bowl with the butter, eggs, and sour cream.

Place in a greased casserole dish and bake at 350 degrees fer' about an hour.

I got My Eye On My Sister Casserole –

- 2 cans chopped Spam
- 1 can diced tomatoes
- 1 cup water
- 1 cup uncooked elbow macaroni
- 1 can tomato sauce
- 1 chopped onion
- 1 teaspoon garlic salt
- 1 teaspoon black pepper

Brown the meat and onion. Add the rest of the ingredients. Bring to a boil.

Add the macaroni and simmer fer' about 30 minutes.

Mom's Got A Tongue Ring Spam Patties –

- 2 cans Spam, ground
- ¼ cup cold water
- ½ teaspoon garlic salt
- ½ teaspoon black pepper
- 4 slices Mozzarella cheese
- 1 can spaghetti sauce
- ½ cup flour
- 1 beaten egg
- ¼ cup breadcrumbs
- 1 tablespoon oil
- 1 tablespoon minced parsley

Mix the meat, water, garlic salt, and pepper in a large bowl.
Make 4 patties out of mixture. Coat the patties on both sides with flour, then dip in the egg, roll in the breadcrumbs.

Brown patties in oil and place patties in a baking dish. Top with cheese. Pour spaghetti sauce over all and bake at 400 degrees fer' about 30 minutes.

Bubba's Spam Bake –

- 3 cans Spam, sliced
- 1 teaspoon garlic salt
- 2 tablespoons melted butter
- 1 cup crushed cornflakes (WIC will cover this)
- $\frac{1}{2}$ cup evaporated milk
- 1 teaspoon pepper

Dip Spam slices in milk and roll in cornflake crumbs.

Place coated meat in a large casserole dish and season with garlic salt and pepper.

Spoon melted butter over meat. Bake fer' about an hour at 350 degrees.

<u>Mom, Dad's In Jail Again Quick Meal -</u>

- 1 box long grain wild rice
- 2 cans chopped Spam
- 1 cup chopped celery
- 2 cans chicken rice soup
- 1 cup chopped onions
- 12 torn slices of toast

Cook the rice as directed on package. Cook the Spam meat, onions, celery, and drain.

Break toast; add rice, meat mixture, and soup. Put mixture in a large casserole dish and bake at 350 degrees fer' about an hour.

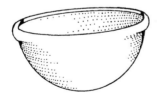

Your defiantly Trailer Trash If:

➢ Somebody tells you that you've got something in your teeth and you take them out to see what it is.

➢ You missed 6th grade graduation because you had jury duty.

➢ You think a quarter horse is that ride in front of K-Mart.

➢ You've used a toilet brush as a back scratcher.

➢ You've asked the preacher "How's it hangin'?"

➤ You go to the family reunion to pick up chicks.

➤ You mow your lawn and find a car.

➤ You carry a can of paint to defend your sister's honor.

➤ Your father walks you to school because you are in the same grade.

➤ You've ever drunk mouthwash just because you're too lazy to walk down to the liquor store.

➤ Your baseball bat "ain't never been used on a ball, but it's sure hit plenty of other things."

➢ You've ever shot a mouse inside your home.

➢ Your steps going into the front door falls over and kills more than three dogs.

➢ Your home has more miles on it than your car.

➢ Your Christmas tree is still up in February.

➢ You think potted meat on a saltine is an hors d'ouvre.

➢ You've totaled every car you've ever owned and they are all in your front yard.

➤ You have a homemade fur coat.

➤ Momma taught you how to flip a cigarette.

➤ There has ever been a crime-scene tape on your front door.

➤ You consider a six-pack and a bug-zapper high-quality entertainment.

➤ The taillight covers of your car are made of tape.

➤ Your car has never had a full tank of gas.

The Cops Are Here Again Spam Meat Snacks –

- 1 can sliced Spam
- 8 ounces cream cheese
- 1 Tablespoon milk
- 1 teaspoon garlic powder
- $\frac{1}{4}$ teaspoon celery powder
- $\frac{3}{4}$ teaspoon Worcestershire sauce

Combine all, except Spam and mix until smooth. Spread over Spam slices and serve.

Muffins –

- 1 small jar Old English Cheese
- 1 ½ tablespoons mayonnaise
- 1 stick butter
- 1 can Spam, ground
- ½ teaspoon garlic powder
- ½ teaspoon onion salt
- 8 English muffins, split & toasted

Combine softened cheese and butter; add the remaining ingredients.

Spread on toasted muffins and broil until warm, then cut into quarters and serve.

Trailer Park Style Mac & Cheese –

- 1 can creamed corn
- 1 can whole kernel corn (do not drain)
- 1 can diced Spam
- 1 can milk
- 1 can cubed government cheese
- 1 can elbow macaroni (dry)

The corn can will be used to measure the ingredients. In a large bowl combine a can of each ingredient.

Pour combined ingredients into a large casserole dish.
Stir several times during cooking. Bake at 375 degrees, uncovered fer' about45 minutes.

After baking let stand fer' about 15 minutes to thicken.

They Shut The Power Off Again Casserole -

- 4 cups sliced carrots
- $\frac{1}{4}$ stick butter
- 1 chopped onion
- 1 cup cubed government cheese
- 1 cup cubed Spam

Combine all the ingredients and put into a large casserole dish.

Cover with crushed potato chips and bake at 350 degrees fer' about 35 minutes.

Sit On My Lab Darlin' Sauerkraut Casserole -

- 1 can chopped Spam
- 1 large can sauerkraut
- 2 cans drained tomato wedges
- 1 chopped onion
- $\frac{1}{2}$ cup brown sugar
- 6 slices crisp fried bacon

Mix all the ingredients together in a large bowl. Place mixture into a large casserole dish and bake at 350 degrees fer' about an hour.

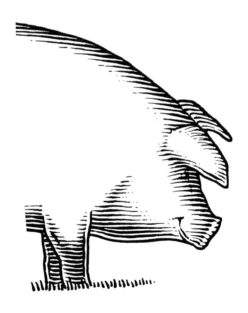

You Are Most Defiantly Trailer Trash If:

➤ Your bathroom deodorizer is a box of kitchen matches.

➤ You keep empty beer cans in your fridge for your friends that don't drink.

➤ The Halloween pumpkin on your front steps has more teeth than your wife.

➤ You think taking a bubble bath starts with eating beans fer' dinner.

➤ Your wife howls at the moon more than your huntin' dogs.

➤ The same pair of boots has been in your family for five generations and they're only twenty years old.

➤ You go swimming with the kids in the drainage ditch behind your trailer.

➤ You think the Franklin Mint is a breath freshener.

➤ Your only tie is made of leather, silver, and turquoise.

➤ You've ever paid for a six-pack of beer with pennies.

➤ Your dog passes gas and you claim it.

➤ You think "loading the dishwasher" means getting your wife drunk.

➤ None of your shirts cover your stomach.

➤ Your stereo speakers used to belong to the Moonlight Drive-in Theater.

➤ Chiggers are included on your list of top 5 hygiene concerns.

➤ Your entire family has ever sat around waiting for a call from the Governor to spare a loved one.

Soups, Stews, And Chowder's

Soups and stews, yea buddy! Now these here are the vittles made for the King and Queen of the park.

So grab one of those stepdaughters and give her a squeeze, hell, you might even get her to wash the dishes, (if she ain't too drunk!)

Free Cheese Soup –

- 6 cups water
- 4 cups chicken broth
- 3 cups diced potatoes
- 1 cup chopped celery
- 1 cup chopped onions
- 2 cans cream of chicken soup
- 1 package mixed vegetables
- $\frac{1}{2}$ pound free cheese

Combine the first five ingredients and boil fer' about 25 minutes. Add the veggies and continue boiling fer' about 10 more minutes.

Add the chicken soup and free cheese; cook until the cheese is melted.

Mom's Out On Bail, Free Cheese Soup –

- 1 ½ quarts chicken broth
- ½ cup carrots
- 2 tablespoons grated carrots
- 2 tablespoons grated onions
- 1 teaspoon salt
- 1 teaspoon pepper
- ½ teaspoon paprika
- 6 tablespoons flour
- 6 tablespoons butter (government issued)
- 1 ½ pints milk
- ½ pound free cheese
- 1 tablespoon Worcestershire sauce

Bring the chicken broth to a boil and add the salt. Stir together butter and flour until smooth and add to the broth, stirring constantly.

Add the milk and bring to boiling point. Add the cheese and Worcestershire sauce.

Simmer until the cheese is melted.

Spam Chowder -

- 3 cups diced Spam
- 1 cup chopped onions
- 2 cups cubed potatoes
- 1 cup cubed carrots
- 1 tablespoon butter
- 2 cups water
- 1 package buttermilk salad dressing
- 2 cups milk

Sauté Spam, onions, potatoes, and carrots in a large pan fer' about 5 minutes.

Add water, cover, and simmer on low fer' about 20 minutes or until the veggies are tender.

Combine salad dressing mix and milk and mix thoroughly. Stir into Spam and veggies.
Bring to a boil, and then reduce the heat. Cover and simmer fer' about 10 minutes.

Meat And Tatter Soup -

- 1 can diced Spam
- $\frac{1}{2}$ cup chopped onions
- $\frac{1}{2}$ cup chopped celery
- 1 package au gratin potato mix
- 2 cups water
- 2 cans cream of celery soup
- 4 cups milk

Brown Spam; remove and drain. Sauté onions and celery in drippings until tender.

Add the potatoes, reserving seasoning pack and mix.
Add water, cover and simmer fer' about 25 minutes, stirring frequently.

Add soup, milk, Spam, and seasonings to potatoes and let simmer fer' about 20 more minutes.

Trailer Tatter Soup –

- 2 cups boiling water
- 2 cups diced potatoes
- $\frac{1}{2}$ cup diced carrots
- $\frac{1}{2}$ cup diced celery
- $\frac{1}{2}$ cup diced onions
- 1 teaspoon salt
- 1 teaspoon pepper
- $\frac{1}{4}$ cup butter
- $\frac{1}{4}$ cup flour
- 2 cups milk
- 1 cup cubed free cheese
- 1 cup bacon (fried and crumbled)

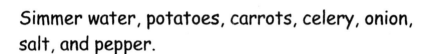

Simmer water, potatoes, carrots, celery, onion, salt, and pepper.

Don't drain. Make a white sauce with butter, flour, milk, and cheese.

Mix together the white sauce and veggies. Top with the crumbled bacon just before serving.

You Are Absolutely Trailer Trash If:

➤ Your grandmother has ever been asked to leave the bingo hall because of her language.

➤ You've ever given rattraps as gifts.

➤ You clean your fingernails with a stick.

➤ Your coffee table used to be a cable spool.

➤ You think a subdivision is part of a math problem.

➢ You've ever bathed with flea and tick soap.

➢ You think "taking out the trash" means taking your in-laws to a movie.

➢ Your kids take a siphon hose to "Show and tell."

➢ You think a hot tub is a stolen bathroom fixture.

➢ Your toilet paper has page numbers on it.

➢ You own more than three shirts with the sleeves cut off.

➤ Your pocketknife often doubles as a toothpick.

➤ You own a denim leisure suit.

➤ Your dog has a litter of puppies on the living room floor and nobody notices.

➤ The dog can't watch you eat without gagging.

➤ You cut your toenails in front of company.

➤ You've ever heard a sheep bleat and had romantic thoughts.

➤ Your mother keeps a spit cup on the ironing board.

➤ The most commonly heard phrase at your family reunion is "What the hell are you looking at?"

➤ You have a rag for a gas cap (on a car that does run).

➤ You have lost at least one tooth opening a beer bottle.

➤ Your wife has a beer belly and you find it attractive.

Popeye Soup –

- 6 tablespoons butter
- 1 cup chopped onions
- 5 cups chicken broth
- 2 diced potatoes
- 2 sliced carrots
- $\frac{1}{4}$ cup raw rice
- 1 package frozen chopped spinach
- 1 teaspoon salt
- 1 pint half & half

Simmer the onions and butter; add carrots, potatoes, rice, and broth.

Boil until the veggies are tender. Add the spinach and half & half.

Simmer fer' about 20 minutes and serve.

Hamburger Stew –

- 1 pound ground beef
- 1 tablespoon butter
- 1 sliced onion
- 1 teaspoon salt
- 1 teaspoon pepper
- 1 tablespoon steak sauce
- 1 can tomatoes
- 3 sliced potatoes
- 3 sliced carrots
- 2 stalks diced celery

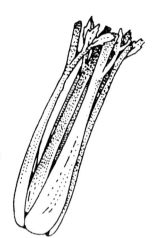

Brown beef lightly in butter, stirring with fork to break up the meat.

Add onion; cook fer' about 5 more minutes and add the remaining ingredients.

Bring mixture to a boil; simmer, covered, fer' about 30 minutes or until the veggies are done.

Serve on top of buttermilk biscuits.

White Trash Chili –

- 2 pounds dried Northern beans
- 1 ½ cups diced onion
- 1 tablespoon olive oil
- 1 tablespoon oregano
- 2 teaspoons cumin
- 1 teaspoon seasoned salt
- 1 teaspoon cayenne
- 4 ½ quarts chicken broth
- 8 boned and skinned chicken breast halves
- 8 ounces can green chilies

Place beans in a saucepan, cover with water, and bring to a boil.
Drain and rinse beans.

In a 5-quart Dutch oven, sauté the onions in oil until tender.
Combine oregano, cumin, salt, and cayenne pepper. Divide in half.

Stir half of the seasoning mixture into the onions.

Add beans, broth, and garlic. Coat chicken with the remaining seasoning mixture.

Place chicken in a large baking dish. Bake the chicken in a 350 degree oven fer' about 15 minutes.

Cube the chicken and add it to the beans. Stir in the chilies and simmer fer' about 2 hours.

Sugar Britches Ham & Bean Soup –

- 1 pound soup beans (soaked overnight)
- 2 pounds ham hocks
- 10 cups water
- 8 ounces tomato sauce
- 3 beef bouillon cubs
- 14 ounces chopped stewed tomatoes
- 6 chopped carrots
- 5 cubed potatoes
- 1 tablespoon minced garlic
- 1 large chopped onion
- 2 bay leaves
- 2 tablespoons parsley
- 1 tablespoon salt
- 1 tablespoon black pepper
- 1 teaspoon thyme

Combine all the ingredients in a large pot. Simmer on low heat fer' about 6 hours.

Remove the ham hocks from the pot. Cut off the meat and return to soup. Remove the bay leaves before serving.

Who's Your Daddy! No Really, Who Is Your Daddy? Crawdad Gumbo –

- 10 ounce small cubed salt pork
- 1 tablespoon flour
- 1 chopped onion
- 2 cups water
- ½ pound fresh okra
- 8 ounces frozen corn
- 1 can whole tomatoes
- 1 teaspoon parsley flakes
- 1 teaspoon cayenne
- 1 teaspoon smoked salt
- 1 teaspoon white pepper
- 1 pint half and half
- 1 pound cooked crawfish tail meat

In a large skillet, fry the salt pork until browned. Remove the salt pork from skillet and stir the flour into the drippings.

Add the onion and cook, stirring often, until slightly brown.

Add the water, pork, okra, corn, tomatoes, and seasonings.

Simmer fer' about 25 minutes. Add the half and half and crawfish and simmer fer' about 15 more minutes.

How To Talk Trailer Trash

HEIDI – noun. Greeting.

HIRE YEW – Complete sentence. Remainder of greeting. Usage: *Heidi, hire yew?*

BARD – verb. Past tense of the infinitive "to borrow." Usage: *"My brother bard my pickup truck."*

MUNTS – noun. A calendar division. Usage: *"My brother from Jawjuh bard my pickup truck and ain't herd from him in munts."*

THANK – verb. Ability to cognitively process. Usage: *"Ah thank ah'll have a bare."*

BARE – noun. An alcoholic beverage made of barley, hops, and yeast. Usage: *"Ah thank ah'll have a bare."*

RANCH – noun. A tool used for tight'nin' bolts. Usage: *"I thank I left my ranch in the back of that pickup truck my brother from Jawjuh bard a few munts ago.*

ALL – noun. A petroleum-based lubricant. Usage: *"I sure hope my brother from Jawjuh puts all in my pickup truck."*

FAR – noun. A conflagration. Usage: *"If my brother from Jawjuh don't change the all in my pickup truck, that thing's gonna catch far."*

TAR – noun. A rubber wheel. Usage: *"Gee, I hope that brother of mine from Jawjuh don't get a flat tar in my pickup truck.*

TIRE – noun. A tall monument. Usage: *"Lord willin' and the creek don't rise, I sure do hope to see that Eiffel Tire in Paris sometime."*

RETARD – Verb. To stop working. Usage: *"My grampaw retard at age 65."*

FAT – noun, verb. 1. A battle or combat. 2. To engage in battle or combat. Usage: *"You younguns keep fat'n, n' ah'm gonna whup y'uh.*

RATS – noun. Entitled power or privilege. Usage: *"We pour people are willin' to fat for are rats."*

FARN – adjective. Not local. Usage: *"I cuddint unnerstand a wurd he sed…mus' be from some farn country."*

DID – adjective. Not alive. Usage: *"He's did, Jimmy."*

EAR – noun. A colorless, odorless gas: Oxygen. Usage: *"He cain't breathe…give 'im some ear!"*

HAZE – a contraction. Usage: *"Is Bubba smart?"* *"Nah…haze ignert."*

Man I'm Tore Up Chili –

- 1 pound ground beef
- 1 tablespoon butter (government)
- $\frac{1}{2}$ cup chopped onion
- $\frac{1}{2}$ cup chopped green pepper
- 2 tablespoons minced garlic
- 3 chopped chili peppers
- 6 ounces tomato paste
- 1 can kidney beans (un-drained)
- 2 cans chili beans (un-drained)
- 1 cup shredded cheese (government)

Brown beef in a large skillet. Drain fat and set aside.

In a large pot, cook vegetables in butter until soft.
Add the tomato paste, chili powder, beans, and browned beef to pot.

Simmer soup over low heat fer' about 3 hours.
Stir the cheese into the chili immediately before serving.

Da' Man Keepin' Us Down Beef Noodle Soup –

- 2 pounds boneless beef, cubed
- 2 tablespoons oil
- 2 teaspoon onion salt
- 1 teaspoon garlic salt
- ½ cup white vinegar
- 1 cup beef broth
- 1 ½ quarts water
- 1 pound egg noodles, unprepared

In a large, ovenproof skillet, brown beef cubes in the oil and salts.

Simmer fer' about 5 minutes and add the water and beef broth.
Cover the pan and place in a 350 degree oven fer' about 2 hours.

Remove from oven, bring to a boil on stovetop, and add the noodles. Boil fer' about 20 more minutes and serve.

Tinker's Taco Soup –

- 1 pound hamburger (Church Pantry)
- 24 ounces tomato juice
- 2 cans dark kidney beans (un-drained)
- 1 can sweet corn (un-drained)
- 1 package taco seasoning mix

Cook and drain the hamburger. Put all the ingredients in a large saucepan and let simmer on low fer' about 2 hours.

Serve over corn chips and top with shredded free cheese.

Soup Line Creamy Onion Soup –

- 1 ¼ cups chicken broth
- 3 tablespoons corn starch
- 1 can cream of onion soup
- 1 can cream of chicken soup
- 1 can cream of celery soup
- ¼ cup shredded Mozzarella cheese
- ¼ cup shredded free cheese
- ¼ cup shredded Provolone cheese

In a large blender, combine broth and cornstarch.
In the top pan of a double boiler over medium heat, combine broth mixture with the soups. Mix well.

When heated through, stir in the cheese and heat until melted.
Pour into oven proof bowls and broil in the oven until the tops ate lightly browned.

Serve warm with bread or biscuits.

Call Someone Who Cares Potato Carrot Soup –

- 1 chopped onion
- ½ cup butter (government)
- 3 cups water
- 2 chicken bouillon cubes
- 1 bay leaf
- 1 teaspoon celery salt
- 1 teaspoon garlic salt
- 3 diced potatoes
- 1 cup thinly sliced carrots
- ¼ cup water
- 2 tablespoons flour
- 1 can evaporated milk

In a large pot, sauté the onions in butter until the onions are clear but not brown.
Add the water, bouillon, bay leaf, celery salt, garlic salt, potatoes, and carrots to the pot.
Simmer until potatoes and carrots are tender and combine water and flour to the pot.

Simmer fer' 15 more minutes and serve!

Yo MAMA SO POOR..

- **She bounces food stamps!**

- **She can't afford to live in a two-story Cheerio box!**

- **She can't afford to pay attention!**

- **She went to McDonald's and put a milkshake on layaway.**

- **Your family ate cereal with a fork to save milk.**

- **Burglars break into her trailer and leave money.**

- **Yo Mamma so poor she can't afford the o or the r.**

- I saw her kicking a beer can down the street, I asked her what she was doing, she said "Moving."

- When she goes to KFC, she has to lick other people's fingers!!

- When I ring the doorbell she says, "DING."

- Her face is on the front of a food stamp.

- When she heard about the "Last Supper", she thought she had ran out of food stamps.

- She was in K-Mart with a box of Hefty bags. I said, "What ya doin'? She said, "Buying luggage."

- She waves around a Popsicle stick and calls it air conditioning.

- You ask her where the facilities are, and she say, "Pick a corner, any corner."

- I walked into your trailer and 3 roaches tripped me and tried to take my wallet!

- I stepped on a cigarette in her trailer house and she said, "Who turned off the heat?"

Sad But True!!!

A trailer trash woman went down to the Welfare Office to get aid. The office worker asked her, "How many children do you have?" "Ten, " she replied. "What are their names?" he asked.

"Johnny, Johnny, Johnny, Johnny, Johnny, Johnny, Johnny, Johnny, Johnny, and Johnny, " she answered.

"They're all named Johnny?" he asked. "What if you want them to come in from playing outside?"

"Oh, that's easy, " she said. "I just call Johnny, " and they all come running in."

"And, if you want them to come to the table for dinner?"
"I just say, "Johnny, come eat your dinner, " she answered.

"But what if you want to call just one particular one of your kids?"

"Oh, in that case, I'll have to use the kid's last name."

Trailer Trash Recipes Using
HOT DOGS!

Next to government issues butter on a cracker, ain't too much out there in the food chain cheaper than good old hot dogs!

Oh yea, them trailer trash folks love their hot dogs.

This next chapter will enlighten you with the fine gourmet tactics of cookin' up vittles with the classy meat known by many names, such as: Wieners, Dogs, Franks, Rolled heavens, Packaged pride, Little piggy's and my favorite, Tube Steak!

So get to the kitchen, open the fridge, grab a beer and get ready to serve your quests a mouth full of tube steak!!!! (Can I say that?)

Bubba's Bean Meal –

- 1 $\frac{1}{2}$ teaspoons yellow mustard
- 1/3 cup BBQ sauce
- $\frac{1}{4}$ cup brown sugar
- 2 cans baked beans
- 1 package hot dogs

Mix all the ingredients together in an ovenproof casserole dish.

Bake at 350 degrees fer' about 25 minutes.

Billy Ray's BBQ Hot Dogs –

- $\frac{3}{4}$ cup chopped onions
- 3 tablespoons butter (government)
- 1 $\frac{1}{2}$ cups chopped celery
- 1 $\frac{1}{2}$ cups ketchup
- $\frac{3}{4}$ cup water
- 1/3 cup lemon juice
- 3 tablespoons brown sugar
- 3 tablespoons vinegar
- 1 tablespoon Worcestershire sauce
- 1 tablespoon yellow mustard
- 2 packages hot dogs
- 16 hot dog buns

In a saucepan over medium heat, sauté the onion in butter until tender.

Add the celery, ketchup, water, lemon juice, sugar, vinegar, Worcestershire sauce, and mustard; bring to a boil.

Reduce heat; cover and simmer fer' about 30 minutes.
 Cut three $\frac{1}{4}$ inch slits on each side of hot dogs; place in a casserole dish and pour the sauce over the dogs.

Cover and bake at 350 degrees fer' about 45 minutes or until the dogs are heated through.

Serve on the hot dog buns!

Granny's Skillet Dogs –

- 1 can cream of celery soup
- $\frac{3}{4}$ cup water
- 1 tablespoon butter (government)
- 1 package hot dogs, cut into $\frac{1}{2}$ inch pieces
- $\frac{3}{4}$ cup uncooked rice
- 1 package frozen peas
- 5 ounces sliced mushrooms
- 1 cup shredded cheese (government)

In a large skillet, combine the soup, water, and butter; bring to a boil.

Add the hot dogs and rice. Reduce heat; cover and simmer fer' about 20 minutes.
Stir in the peas and mushrooms. Cover and simmer fer' about 20 minutes or until the peas are tender.

Sprinkle with cheese; cover and let stand until melted.

Trailer Dogs –

- 8 hot dogs
- 2 cups mashed potatoes
- $\frac{1}{2}$ teaspoon dry mustard
- $\frac{1}{2}$ cup grated cheese (government)
- 1 teaspoon paprika

Split hot-dogs the long way not quite all the way through.

Fill the split opening with mashed potatoes mixed with the dry mustard.
Sprinkle the top with paprika. Bake in a 375 degree oven fer' about 15 minutes or until slightly browned on top.

Top with grated free cheese and serve!

Welfare hash –

- 6 hot dogs
- 6 cubed potatoes
- 1 chopped onion
- $\frac{1}{2}$ teaspoon salt
- $\frac{1}{2}$ teaspoon pepper
- $\frac{1}{2}$ teaspoon garlic powder

Par boil the potato cubes until they are slightly tender when poked with a fork.

Slice the hot dogs into chunks. Heat a coating of oil in a large frying pan. Add the onion, hot dogs, and potato cubes.

Cook until the potatoes are golden and serve!

You Are Seasoned Trailer Trash When:

➢ You rip a loud one and blame your date.

➢ You know you daddy's C.B. handle, but not his real name.

➢ Your bowling ball cost more than your collage education.

➢ You've talked to your mama on the C.B., but have never met her in person.

➢ The sound of a siren sends your family running for the woods.

➢ You shave your armpits with your husband's fishing knife.

➢ The cottage cheese container in your refrigerator holds night crawlers.

- You drive 600 miles to see an image of Elvis that has miraculously appeared in water stains on the ceiling of a trailer.

- Your chili's secret ingredient comes from a bait shop.

- Your retirement plans include getting your own place.

- None of the tires on your car are the same size.

- The morning after your kid's slumber party, the dogs have fleas.

- Turning on your lights involves pulling a string.

- Your handkerchief doubles as your shirtsleeve.

- You go to your sister's wedding just to kiss the bride.

- You've ever used a Laundromat as a mailing address.

- You've ever given yourself a social disease.

- All of your relatives would have to die to wipe out illiteracy.

- There is more oil in your baseball cap than in your car.

- You've ever water-skied in your underwear.

- You've ever been on television not wearing a shirt.

- Your most expensive shoes have numbers on the heels.

Zed's Hot Dog Soup –

- 1 pounds hot dogs
- 1 tablespoon vegetable oil
- 1 cup chopped onion
- 1 cup chopped celery
- 2 cups sliced carrots
- 2 minced garlic cloves
- 6 cups water
- 2 cans chicken broth
- 1 pound lentils
- 1 teaspoon salt
- 1 teaspoon black pepper
- 1 teaspoon chopped basil

Cut the hot dogs into 1-inch pieces. In a large soup pot, sauté the hot dogs in the oil until browned.

Remove hot dogs and sauté the onion, celery, carrots, and garlic fer' about 10 minutes.

Add the water, stock, lentils, salt, pepper, and basil.

Bring to a boil, then reduce the heat to low and simmer fer' about 2 hours.

Adjust the seasonings and add the cooked hot dogs back to the soup.

Free Cheese Roll Ups –

- 30 cocktail franks
- 10 slices of free cheese
- 2 packages of Crecent rolls

Take the roll dough and unroll them carefully.
Cut each triangle in half; keeping the triangular
shape.

Then wrap 1/3 or a piece of cheese around the
frank and holding it with your fingers start
rolling it in the roll.

Start at the large end of the triangle and roll
towards the tip.
Bake fer' about 10 minutes in a 400 degree oven.

Uncle Maynard's Weiner?? –

- 1 hot dog
- 1 hot dog bun
- 2 paper towels
- Heavy duty aluminum foil
- 1-quart size cardboard milk carton.

Wet the paper towels and wring them out, put hot dog in bun and wrap the whole thing up in the paper towels, covering the ends.

Wrap this in the foil, be careful not to wrap to tightly.
Place in the milk carton, take outside and light the milk carton with a match.

This is done when the milk carton is gone.

Breakfast Doggie Style –

- 1 package chopped hot dogs
- 2 teaspoons sugar
- 3 teaspoons soy sauce
- $\frac{1}{2}$ cup sliced onions
- $\frac{1}{2}$ cup sliced green peppers
- 8 beaten eggs
- 8 Kaiser rolls, sliced and toasted

Heat a heavy nonstick skillet over medium high heat.

Cook the dogs until browned. Stir in the next four ingredients and pepper to taste.

Cover and cook fer' about 4 minutes, until the veggies are almost tender.
Stir in the eggs and cook and stir until the eggs are set.

Serve the egg mixture over toasted rolls.

Food Stamp Casserole –

- 3 tablespoons oil
- 1 ½ cups sliced onions
- 1 pound diced hot dogs
- 2 cups cooked rice
- 11 ounces cream of mushroom soup
- 6 slices free cheese

Preheat the oven to 350 degrees. Heat the oil in a large skillet and sauté the onions until tender.

Add the hot dogs and brown lightly. Stir in the next three ingredients and salt and pepper to taste.

Cook fer' about 5 more minutes and transfer to a baking dish, top with cheese and bake fer' about 15 minutes.

Non Workin' Man's Lunch –

- 2 quarts of water
- 4 ears of corn
- 1 head cabbage, cut into wedges
- 1 package hot dogs

Combine all the ingredients into a Dutch oven.
Simmer fer' about 30 minutes.

Drain and serve!

Who Did That? Frank & Ham Bake –

- 3 ounces macaroni
- 2 tablespoon olive oil
- $\frac{1}{2}$ cup chopped onion
- $\frac{1}{2}$ pound ham chunks
- $\frac{1}{2}$ pound chopped hot dogs
- 3 tablespoons chopped parsley
- 1 can tomatoes, chopped and drained
- $\frac{1}{2}$ pound shredded free cheese
- $\frac{1}{2}$ cup diced green peppers
- $\frac{1}{2}$ cup sliced zucchini

Preheat the oven to 350 degrees. Cook the macaroni in a large pan of boiling water fer' about 10 minutes. Drain and set aside. Heat oil in a large skillet over medium heat.

Sauté the onion, ham, and hot dogs fer' about 5 minutes. Add the parsley, tomatoes and their juice.

Cook fer' about 5 minutes and stir in half the cheese, macaroni, bell pepper, and zucchini. Transfer to a lightly oiled casserole dish. Top with the remaining cheese and bake fer' about 20 minutes.

Doggie Bread –

- 1 ½ cup cornmeal
- 1 ½ cup flour
- 4 teaspoons baking powder
- ¼ cup sugar
- 2 eggs
- 1 cup milk
- 6 strips bacon
- 1 package hot dogs
- 1 cup whole corn
- ¼ cup diced green peppers
- ¼ cup diced onions

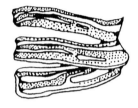

Preheat the oven to 400 degrees. Sauté the bacon, hot dogs, peppers, and onions over low heat, until lightly brown.

Stir in the cornmeal, flour, baking powder, and sugar in a large bowl. Add the eggs and milk, whipping with a wire whisk until smooth.

Grease a large baking pan and stir hot mixture into cornmeal mixture, then pour into the greased pan.
Bake fer' about 45 minutes or until done. If the bread browns prematurely, cover with foil for the final few minutes to prevent further darkening.

Top with hot chili and serve!

Trailer Trash Family Tree

Many, many years ago when I was
twenty three,
I got married to a widow who was
pretty as could be.

This widow had a grown-up daughter.
Who had hair of red.
My father fell in love with her, and
soon the two were wed.

This made my dad my son-in-law, and
changed my very life.
My daughter was my mother, for she
was my father's wife.

To complicate the matters worse,
although it brought me joy. I soon
became the father, of a bouncing baby
boy.

My little baby then became a brother –
in-law to dad. And so became my uncle,
though it made me very sad. For if he

was my uncle, then that also made him
brother. To the widow's grown-up
daughter, who, of course, was my step
mother.

Father's wife then has a son, who kept
them on the run.
For he was my daughter's son. My wife
is now my mother's mother, and it
makes me blue.
Because, although she is my wife, she's
my grandma too.

If my wife is my grandmother, then I
am her grandchild.
And every time I think of it, it simply
drives me wild.

For now I have become the strangest
case you ever saw.
As the husband of my grandmother, I
am my own grandpa!!!!

Trailer Trash Recipes Using Macaroni And Free Government Cheese!

When it comes to trailer trash recipes, then good old mac and cheese has to be on the menu!

Why, mac & free cheese go together with trailer trash, like stink on a skunk. Hell, you can feed yourself and the eight kids and step kids fer' about two bucks in food stamps!

Sister Sib's Baked Macaroni & Cheese -

- 1 ½ cups elbow macaroni
- 2 tablespoons butter (government)
- 2 tablespoons flour
- ¼ cup milk
- 1 cup cream
- ¼ teaspoon paprika
- ½ teaspoon white pepper
- 2 ½ cups grated free cheese
- 1 teaspoon salt

Preheat the oven to 350 degrees. Boil the macaroni according to the package directions; drain and set aside.

Meanwhile, melt butter in a saucepan over low heat and blend in the flour, stirring constantly. Gradually stir in milk and cream. Cook, stirring constantly, until the mixture boils and thickens, about three minutes.

Remove from the heat and add paprika, pepper, and 2 cups of free cheese; stir until the cheese is melted.
Gently stir in the macaroni and salt to taste.
Place in a buttered casserole dish.

Garnish the top with the remaining $\frac{1}{2}$ cup of free cheese and dot with additional butter.
Bake fer' about 30 minutes and serve to them kids!

I Heard Dat' Macaroni And Cheese –

- $\frac{1}{2}$ pound macaroni
- 1 cup shredded free cheese
- 3 tablespoons government butter
- 1 teaspoon salt
- $\frac{1}{2}$ teaspoon cayenne
- $\frac{1}{2}$ cup milk
- 1 egg
- $\frac{1}{2}$ cup breadcrumbs

Cook the macaroni according to the package directions.
Blanch the cooked macaroni in cold water to prevent sticking.

Cover the bottom of a baking dish with a layer of macaroni, a sprinkle of cheese, bits of butter, salt and pepper.

Continue until all is used, having cheese on top.
Mix the milk and egg together, pour over the
dish, cover top with crumbs, bake in moderate
oven long enough to brown top and cook egg and
milk.

Serve hot right from the dish!

Billy's Beer Belly Pasta –

- 3 cups spiral pasta
- 2/3 cup milk
- 1 pound cubed free cheese
- $\frac{1}{4}$ teaspoon dry mustard
- $\frac{1}{2}$ teaspoon turmeric
- $\frac{1}{2}$ teaspoon garlic salt
- $\frac{1}{2}$ teaspoon black pepper

Cook the pasta according to the package directions and drain well.

While the pasta is cooking, put the remaining ingredients in the top of double boiler over simmering water.

Stir with a wire whisk until smooth. Keep the cheese mixture warm until the pasta is cooked and drained.
Stir the pasta into the cheese mixture and serve!

Trailer Lovin' Mac & Cheese –

- 2 quarts water
- 1 teaspoon salt
- 8 ounces elbow macaroni
- 4 cups shredded free cheese
- 8 ounces sour cream
- 1 cup mayonnaise
- 2 tablespoons chopped onion
- 1 cup crushed cheese crackers

Bring the water to a boil in a large Dutch oven; stir in the macaroni.

Return to a rapid boil; and cook fer' about 10 minutes, or until tender and drain.
Rinse with cold water and drain again.

Combine the macaroni, cheese, and the next 3 ingredients. Spoon into a lightly greased baking dish; sprinkle with the crushed crackers and bake at 325 degrees fer' about 40 minutes.

Unemployment Mac & Free Cheese -

- 1 package elbow macaroni
- 6 tablespoons butter (government)
- 3 tablespoons flour
- 2 cups milk
- 8 ounces cubed cream cheese
- 2 cups shredded free cheese
- 2 teaspoons Dijon mustard
- $\frac{1}{2}$ teaspoon salt
- $\frac{1}{2}$ teaspoon pepper
- $\frac{3}{4}$ cup dry breadcrumbs
- 2 tablespoons parsley

Cook the macaroni according to the package directions.
Meanwhile, melt 4 tablespoons butter in a large saucepan.

Stir in the flour until smooth. Add the milk and bring to a boil; cook and stir fer' about 3 minutes. Reduce the heat; add the cheeses, mustard, salt, and pepper.

Stir until the cheese is melted and the sauce is smooth.

Drain the macaroni; add to the cheese sauce and stir to coat.
Transfer to a greases baking dish. Melt the remaining butter; toss with breadcrumbs and parsley.

Sprinkle over the macaroni. Bake, uncovered, at 400 degrees fer' about 25 minutes or until golden brown.

Cut And Dry, You Are Trailer Trash If:

- You've ever scraped your elbows trying to get something out of the dumpster.

- Your favorite color is shiny.

- You wish you could bend your head down as far as your dog can.

- You know where to get government cheese.

- Your attorney can be reached at 1-800-WIP-LASH.

- Your kids end up on milk cartons before you notice they're missing.

- You've seen someone spray his or her telephone with Lysol after you used it.

- Your kids give meaning to the term "nose mining".

- Your wife asks about layaway at flea markets.

- Your wife breaks her ankle bracelets on your rearview mirror.

- Trash pick up day is a family event!

- Your dad had a real knack for finding things at the dump that were "too damned good" to be thrown away.

- You think a pap smear is what daddy wipes on his jeans after a healthy sneeze.

- The sight of a Slim Jim makes your wife's mouth water.

- You'd rather watch Cops than Seinfeld.

- Your mom and dad shared everything including a set of teeth.

- Your refrigerator has a coat of auto primer on it.

- Your contest entry on "How to avoid the Repo Man" won you a set of jumper cables.

- You pay extra lot rent for the privilege of being within walking distance to the dumpster.

- You smoke fish in your trunk.

- One of your relatives went bankrupt after winning the lottery.

- You buy teeth through the mail.

- Your sister runs a dating service on her C.B. called Trucker Tail.

- You Figure you're entitled to use 7-Eleven as your business address since you use the pay phone and restroom there.

- Your sister's first training bra came from GOOD WILL and had cups the size of basketball hoops.

- You've tried to get credit with your sweepstakes finalist notifications.

- You've ever asked the police if your kids get to keep what they stole.

- You lost interest in your wife after she lost 250 pounds.

- Your outdoor Christmas lights cost more than your trailer did.

- Your dentist can't clean your teeth without gagging.

- You refuse to live in a trailer park that has speed bumps.

- The only thing your wife uses a stem iron on is a grilled cheese sandwiches.

- You've ever tried to buy Girl Scout cookies with food stamps.

- You wrote Dear Abby a letter when your rabbit had baby kittens.

- You've ever sent your husband to the store for a box of CARP-HELPER.

- The high school football team came to your baby shower.

- You think being double – jointed entitles you to additional welfare benefits.

- Your husband's idea of a weakness is the government's idea of a felony.

- Your son Bud is named after what was on tap the night he was born.

- You started your own business with a bucket, a flashlight, and a frog gig.

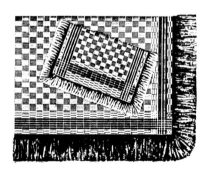

- Your family portrait looks like a science project gone awry.

- You've ever broken a set of knuckles or toes on a vending machine.

- You've ever put a 911 operator on hold while you grabbed a cold one.

- Your dishtowels double as shop rags.

You are to be commended for putting up with 120 pages of this book. Having already wasted the time it took to get this far, you might as well continue.

If it's of any comfort to you, you can plan on it getting worse from this point on.

I hesitate to stray off in the direction of offering you advice and guidance since I am really not qualified to do so.

I would suggest, however, that you might benefit from some introspection on just what kind of person you are .... buying a book like this one. Perhaps there are areas in which you could work on self-improvement.

Unfortunately, you can't get away with blaming someone else, just because someone else might have gotten this book as a gift for you. If that was what happened, you really need to ask yourself why you are the kind of person for whom such a gift is appropriate.

The Editor

A Letter From A Trailer Trash Mother To Her Daughter

Dear Child:
I am writing this slow because I know that you can't read fast.

We don't live where we did when you left home.

Your dad read in the paper that most accidents happen within 20 miles from your home so we moved.

I won't be able to send you the address, as the last family that lived here took the trailer house numbers when they left so that they wouldn't have to change their address.

This place is real nice. It even has a washing machine. I'm not sure it works too well though. Last week I put a load in, pulled the chain, and haven't seen them since.

The weather isn't too bad here; it only rained twice last week. The first time it rained for three days and the second time for four days.

The coat you wanted me to send, your uncle Bubba said it would be a little too heavy to send in the mail with the buttons on, so we cut them off and put them in the pockets.

We got another bill from the funeral home. They said if we don't make the last payment on Grandma's grave, up she comes. Scooter locked his keys in the truck yesterday.
We were worried because it took him two hours to get me and Shelby out.

Your sister had a baby this morning but I haven't found out what it is yet, so I don't know if you're an aunt or an uncle.
If the baby is a girl your sister is gonna name it after me; She's going to call it mom.

Uncle Pete fell in a whiskey vat last week. Some men tried to pull him out before he fought them off and drowned. We had him cremated and he burned for three days.

Three of your friends went off a bridge in a pick-up truck. Ralph was driving. He rolled down the window and swam to safety. Your two friends were in the back. They drowned because they couldn't get the tailgate down.

There isn't much more news at this time. Nothing much as happened.

Love,
Mom

PS – I was going to send you some money but the envelope was already sealed.

The

VEGETARIAN
WILD GAME
COOKBOOK

Recipes for really great dishes using
only those game animals that are

PURELY   VEGETARIAN

See, you can be politically correct without giving up those
great steaks or barbequed stuff . . . . and we know how im-
portant it is for you to be politically correct.

Rick Black

$9.95 plus $3.00 shipping and handling

COOKIN'
WITH
BEER

Anybody can sit there drinkin' beer 'til the cows come home ... or go to work ... or whatever it is that cows do.

The real connisure ...conneusiour ... conus .... the real cool guy is the one who uses beer as an ingredient in cookin'.

You'll find, in this book, some recipes that'll absolutely knock your socks off .... and some other stuff you'll want to keep out of the hands of women, children and Republicans.

By Rick Black

$9.95 plus $3.00 shipping and handling

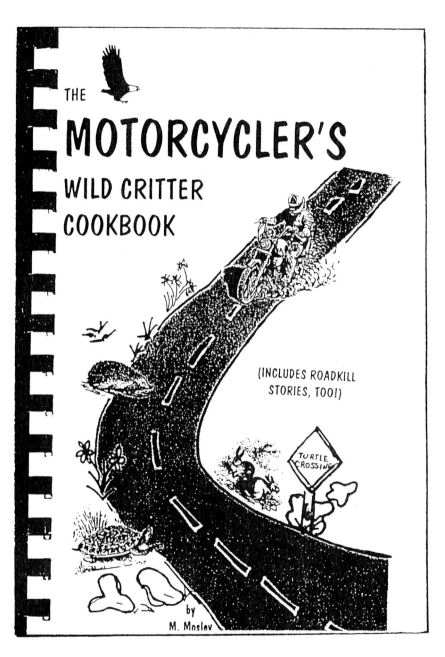

$9.95 plus $3.00 shipping and handling

SOUTHWESTERN NATIVE AMERICAN COOKING

by Barb Soden

$9.95 plus $3.00 shipping and handling

the
TURKEY
COOKBOOK

. . . . all about turkey huntin' &
some knock-your-socks-off recipes

Rick Black

$9.95 plus $3.00 shipping and handling

The

HUNTING

in the

NUDE

COOKBOOK

see page iv for a picture of a nude.

- Flat out Double-Good Wild Game Cookin'
- And some things to think about as you consider stompin' around in fields and forests ... in the nude.

by Bruce Carlson

$9.95 plus $3.00 shipping and handling

The
FUNKY DUCK
Duck COOKBOOK

A REAL HE-MAN COOKBOOK WITH RECIPES
THAT USE DEAD THINGS, AND HOT STUFF,
AND PARTS OF PICKUP TRUCKS.

WITH THIS COOKBOOK, YOU CAN BE
A REAL HE-MAN!

BY RICK BLACK

$9.95 plus $3.00 shipping and handling

THE
GREAT MIDWEST AMERICAN

WILD
CRITTER
COOKBOOK

by Bruce Carlson

$11.95 plus $3.00 shipping and handling

BAG 'EM

and

TAG 'EM

-all about deer huntin'

by Rick Black

$9.95 plus $3.00 shipping and handling

INDIAN
COOKING
COOK BOOK

— according to the practices of the:
LAKOTA
CHIPPEWA
CHEROKEE
OTTOWA
CREE

by Bruce Carlson

$9.95 plus $3.00 shipping and handling

Camp Cookin'

.......because camp cooks need to be immersed in lake water more than in dish water.

Mary Ann Kerl

$9.95 plus $3.00 shipping and handling

Bird Up!

Pheasant
Cookbook
'n more

How to shoot 'em & how to cook 'em . . . . . along with dog care hints, safety, sharing our vision with the kids & other good stuff and . . . . .

we haven't forgotten **Quail & Grouse**. There's some good quail & grouse stuff here too.

By Rick Black

$9.95 plus $3.00 shipping and handling

VENISON
COOKBOOK

**A REAL HE-MAN COOKBOOK WITH RECIPES
THAT USE DEAD THINGS, AND HOT STUFF,
AND PARTS OF PICKUP TRUCKS.**

BY RICK BLACK

$9.95 plus $3.00 shipping and handling

CatfisH

(from C to H)

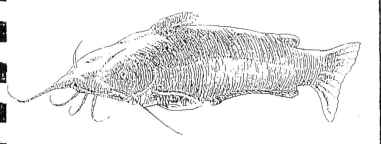

How to Hook 'em
&
How to Cook 'em

This book tells you everything you ever wanted to know about how to catch and how to cook those creatures from the brown lagoon . . . . and probably some stuff you could care less about.

by Rick Black

$9.95 plus $3.00 shipping and handling

TO ORDER COPIES OF:

The Trailer Trash Cookbook . . . .

Please send me _____ copies at $9.95 each plus $3.00 S/H each. (Make checks payable to **QUIXOTE PRESS**.)

Name _____

Street _____

City _____ State _____ Zip _____

SEND ORDERS TO:
QUIXOTE PRESS
3544 Blakslee St.
Wever, IA 52658
800-571-2665

TO ORDER COPIES OF:

The Trailer Trash Cookbook . . . .

Please send me _____ copies at $9.95 each plus $3.00 S/H each. (Make checks payable to **QUIXOTE PRESS**.)

Name _____

Street _____

City _____ State _____ Zip _____

SEND ORDERS TO:
QUIXOTE PRESS
3544 Blakslee St.
Wever, IA 52658
800-571-2665

THE

END